Martin Mooney was born in Belfast and now lives in Co. Antrim. His first collection, *Grub* (Blackstaff Press, 1993; reprinted in the United States by the CavanKerry Press, 2002), won the 1994 Brendan Behan Memorial Award and was shortlisted for the Forward Prize for first collections. His second collection, *Rasputin and His Children*, was recently republished by Lagan Press.

By the same author

Poetry
Grub
Rasputin and His Children

BLUE LAMP DISCO

BLUE LAMP DISCO

MARTIN MOONEY

LAGAN PRESS
BELFAST
2003

Acknowledgements

Some of these poems, or versions of them, have appeared in: *De Brakke Hond* (Belgium), *Dandelion* (Calgary), *The Echo Room Yearbook*, *Fortnight Magazine*, *Matrix* (Montreal), *Outside Left* (a Ha'penny Press pamphlet anthology), *Poetry Ireland Review* and *The Shop*.

'Wind Farm' survives a longer poem first published in *Or Volge L'Anno/At The Year's Turning: An Anthology of Irish Poets Responding to Leopardi* (Dedalus Press, 1998) while 'Ice' outlives a suite of poems set to music as *Near the Western Necropolis* by Ian Wilson and performed by the London Mozart Players in 1999.

'The Ginger Jar' is a response to the painting 'Girl in White' by Louis le Brocquy (Ulster Museum collection) and was included in *A Conversation Piece* (The National Museums and Galleries of Northern Ireland in association with Abbey Press, 2002).

'Spide' appeared in 2001 as a postcard-poem from *Foolscap*, ed. Judi Benson.

Published by
Lagan Press
138 University Avenue
Belfast BT7 1GZ

© Martin Mooney

The moral right of the author has been asserted.

ISBN: 1 904652 07 7
Author: Mooney, Martin
Title: Blue Lamp Disco
2003

Set in Sabon

Cover: 'Holding the Rope' (1986) by Victor Sloan
(*reproduced courtesy of the artist
and the Arts Council of Northern Ireland*)
Printed by Easyprint, Belfast

Contents

The Hoofprint	11
Crowd Scene after *Kung Fu—The Headcrusher*	12
Best Fallers	13
Gospel	14
Blue Lamp Disco	15
Hatchet	16
The Ginger Jar	17
The Pipe-bomber	18
Decommissioning	20
Radio Orange, Radio Drumcree	21
'Why All the Riot Gear for a Nice Weekend?'	22
Day of Action	23
Ceasefire Babies	24
The War Effort	25
Portrait of the Artists	26
On Good Authority	27
The Couple Who Stole My Car	28
Spide	30
Neanderthal Funeral	31
Skateboarders near St. Anne's Cathedral, Belfast	32
Welcome to Dry City	33
Tractatus	35
Read about Ireland's Highest Pub	36
Ice	37
The Spear	38
For Thoth	39
Wind Farm	40
Ringtones	41
The Wreck of the Mobile Library	42
Swarfega	43
Peter Quince	44
Money	45
Marriage	46
Criticism	47
Toilet Training	48
Pet World	49

Special Needs	*50*
The Reconstruction	*51*
The Gallery of Anxiety Will be Closing Shortly	*52*
Why Not Slaughter Your Whole Family?	*53*
The Cancellation of the Races	*54*
One Man Show	*55*
The Naachtun Stela:	
Inscriptions in Time of Civil War	*57*
Fever Diet #2	*58*
Antiquities	*60*
from *The Epic of Gilgamesh*: Enkidu's Dream	*62*
The Last Poem	*63*

The Hoofprint

They say either the Prince of Darkness or the Prince of Orange
left this omega notched or etched in the hump of rock,
a lucky horseshoe for the miners hiking to the Cripple Shaft
to dig lead for the mineral lord and the lord of the soil

to squabble over. Me, I think some joker carved it for a rake,
chiselled it into Cowrie's Craig for poets and gullible souls
and now, like its folk-referents, the incised graffito won't shift
from its outcrop, despite the acid rain, despite erosion.

Crowd Scene after *Kung Fu—the Headcrusher*

Coming soon: *The One-armed Boxer*
and *The Deaf and Dumb Swordswoman*.
We flee the credits as they play 'The Queen'.

We leap from the foyer with one leg extended
in the sham fight of each against each.
We chop and high-kick. We yelp like throaty hens.

In ten years Paisley's Third Force will drill here
and years ago, so many came to glimpse
George Formby in the flesh you couldn't move.

But there are only dozens of us this Saturday,
our heroes badly-dubbed and foreigners
as disproportionately vengeful as ourselves.

Amn't I the Shaolin novice? Aren't you
the quare apprentice from the iceworks,
posed like some animal we don't have here,

the snake, the praying mantis, or the dragon?

Best Fallers

Till we were twelve we played Best Fallers.
You'd nominate the weapon, someone'd mime
a shotgun, knife, bazooka, and you'd fall
as extravagantly, as artfully, as you could.
These were the days when instead of the words
of one popular song, you'd hear people sing
Last night I saw my momma plantin' a bomb,
ooh-eeh, chirpy chirpy cheep-cheep ...
                              Think, then, of boys
doing their best to represent violent death,
throwing out arms and legs and sprawling akimbo
on cindery wasteground. Think of their cries.
I dare you to tell me that all of their efforts were wasted.

Gospel

A shipwracke in the Ardes,
he's lost it on black ice,
folded the Fiat into an elm
and woken to fossil
shellfish shells on Ireland's
ocean-breaking shores.
By the time he crawls uphill
to an all-night bar at dawn,
he's a born-again Christian
who's lost his memory
in the head-on collison.
His worst fears are confirmed
by a voice from the jukebox,
untenable heels, exile—
if it sounds country, well,
it's a country song ...

Blue Lamp Disco

We lay down for 'The Queen'
    and still escaped a kicking
until that Christmas when
    they ambushed us in Mill Street,
loosening my teeth
    and both your bollocks.
You nursed them in our booth
    in Madge's, as we sipped
an underage pint apiece
    and a clunky drum-machine
accompanied the pleas
    of some tinselled cowboy
RUC reservist
    moonlighting on twelve-string,
lachrymose, half-pissed,
    banging on about love.

Hatchet

It wasn't brain surgery, or craftsmanship.
The wood it cut was soft and mackerel-scented,
old fish crates split along the grain for sticks
to light the fire. Old bedroom furniture.

The thing was blunt, but still a hatchet—
in its own way, an instrument of local
and familial piety. My granda had one like it.
So did every hatchet-faced old fishwife

and bookie's runner on the Avenue.
The very word seems made to suit our accent
and our urban folklore. What was buried
back when my Aunt Jane married Buck Alec?

When nostalgia goes armed, it carries a hatchet.

The Ginger Jar

No matter how long and hard
this GI bride

stares past the ginger jar
into the empty air

and the clouds of dust
her ceiling lost

in last night's raid
along the Antrim Road

there will still be people
buried under rubble

and the bombers will return
wing upon wing

whether the porcelain urn
is T'ang, or Ming.

The Pipe-bomber

See your man?
In anyone's hands but his
this bit of DIY'd
blow the hands off you.

Say a child found it
and shook it, say it went off—
where'd you be then?
It's unstable, risky

but a bit of me admires
the cowboy armourer's
persistence in
his shoddy workmanship.

Mostly I think our towns
belong to stubborn
botchers like himself
with the disco moustache

slaving away in the scullery
of an empty flat,
his bag of *Growmore*
open on the worktop.

Any other place he'd be
a boffin hobbyist,
an amateur inventor.
Here, you might as well

just praise him,
might as well say idle
hands and get on with
teaching the kids

to keep their noses out ...
So what if the tradition
of light engineering
has come to this?

There's still the harbour
and boats still leave it.
There's still the airport,
while the weather holds.

Decommissioning

His uncle's last *Action Man*,
stripped of everything
but a crown
of miniature barbed wire,

is pinned, the arms
outstretched, inside the door
of his granny's jakes.

She'll bust a gut.

This nephew gets
a box of cast-off weapons,
tools and uniforms
and half a dozen figures

sprawled in matériel.
'That's lush,' he says. 'That's wheeker.'

Radio Orange, Radio Drumcree

He holds his big white ghetto-blaster,
does the man with the pierced eyebrow,
his boom-box, against a studded ear.

It's clear that it's a huge strain,
a weight his shoulder wasn't ready for.
The tattoo on his neck is crumpled

like a hellfire gospel handout after
the chapel pickets have dispersed.
His closed eyelids are the only smooth

surface on his biting face, twin seas
of concentration or tranquillity.
His is hard listening. His is heavy focus.

'Why All the Riot Gear for a Nice Weekend?'
for Paul Grattan

    The babies' bibs say *Proud to be a Prod* or *Born*
    to Walk the Garvaghy Road.
    When they set up a date for your punishment beating,
    what's the first thought
    goes through your head? If I was you
    I'd be asking myself where a lad might buy
    one of those chocolate-soldier flute band uniforms.
    They say you cope with stagefright by imagining
    your audience naked, but why not pass
    the time by casting a Shankill Road movie
    with Bruce Willis as 'Mad Dog' Johnny Adair?
    And what's the right thing to wear?
    Shorts, I'd say, and a tee-shirt or vest
    with a logo or slogan. Does anyone know the Latin
    for *Simply the Best*?

Day of Action
i.m. Daniel McColgan

It's not a love story, not a scene
from *The Umbrellas of Cherbourg*,
even though it's coming down
in stair-rods. None of us sings

'The Internationale'.
Sooner 'Singin' in the Rain'
or 'We're Here Because We're Here ... '
Everyone's up against the wall.

But look at these comrades kissing—
lovers, workmates, or both?
Are they part of this day of action
that brings Belfast to a standstill

or just an office romance?
No hunger strike rally or Orange
parade would give them such cover.
We're their alibi. They

are licking the salt from our wounds.

Ceasefire Babies

You laughed the day you were born—
though the midwife called it wind
and the labour wards reported
the normal crop of underweights,
some who died, some who went home
with parents who would kill them.
What tickled you so pink?
Maybe the thought of a reunion
arranged by the survivors,
posed for a school photographer
where the Jubilee once stood,
the same smile-making word
in every mouth. *Sestina*, for example.
Maybe *peace*. Or *wean*.

The War Effort
Newtownards, Winter 1919

The aldermen melted the railings down for cannon
then, asked to erect a memorial to the dead, just gurned
about wasting ratepayers' money, suggesting instead
a fire-appliance, the town's first, or a public park;
until a few of the men on the dole and a couple of boys—
there are always corner-boys in an escapade like this—
scraped together a plinth of snow, and a snow-soldier
sporting a tin hat, eyes of nutty slack, and a wooden gun.
The aldermen slapped these ne'er-do-wells in gaol
as vagrants, but were shamed into asking the price
of artillery salvaged from scuttled submarines,
and of limestone and brass, not taking into account
the foundrymen, sculptors and masons who cost, because
their work lasts longer than snow, an arm and a leg.

Portrait of the Artists

We have outlived the sheen and turn-ups
of our Oxfam cast-offs, our army surplus;
outlasted the Brit who stopped us at a turnstile
pointing his SLR at camo'd schoolboys ...
'Where'dja get yer gear, lads—Burton's?'
Arrogant upper-sixth form autodidacts,
we were happy in our demob suits and greatcoats
and made ourselves artists by shoplifting.
We fanned out through the bookshop's yeasty rooms
for *Maldoror* and *A Short History of Surrealism*.
The useless information is our conscience.
The stolen books will educate our children.

On Good Authority

Intern the unloved.
Keep them from touching. Hood them.
Shackle their thin ankles and cuff their thumbs.

It looks on the outside
the way it feels on the inside:
caged, frustrated, boiled dry, paralysed, satanic.

I have it on good authority
that they feel at home
in our weather-beaten compounds.

If I showed you a face you'd say yes,
it's beyond compassion.
You'd as soon kiss a cockroach.

As soon embrace a petrol-soaked bag of spiders
as lift this mujahid from his knees.
He'd be the first to admit

he deserves nothing.
Light-headed with rejection,
dazzled by grief,

he waits (he wants)
to be driven from the arc
-lights of one horizon to the smoking

razor wire of the other.
When we burn this untouchable at the stake,
he'll strike the match.

The Couple Who Stole My Car

have started afresh
on wheels they never got round to paying for.
Part of me wishes them luck,
part of me wants them hurt, especially him
with his greasy quiff
and his brushed-denim drainpipes.

It's her I feel sorry for,
that girlish smile on her face
the day she announced her engagement.
Pure pride at joining the ranks, pure
pleasure, the fuckers.

Oh, I knew her to speak to.
Obese and shabbily dressed,
her millie's swagger
stiff-legged in her leggings.
She was the one did most of the talking.

Why did I share my congratulations?
I might as well have tied tins to the car.
I wish them divorce.

They came to the door
all innocence, asked if I wanted to sell
the *Renault* sitting untaxed at the gate
and like some groom at the altar I said 'I do.'
I told them to take the motor
and sort me out later.
I never saw them again.

It's as if they drove off the face of the earth,

as if I'd imagined them, down
to the last-but-one story she spun me, how
she'd been checking the lottery

with her elderly mum, looked up
to offer a cuppa, and saw
the old dear's false teeth
drop into her lap. 'And that was her dead.'

Which doesn't excuse
what they did. What would? They owe me money.

Spide

You think you're hard. You think I'm fruity,
just because I like my girlfriend's tracksuit,
the way the buttons on the bottoms gape,
exposing thigh and calf. She's got good calves.
Laugh all you like. I'm right, you're wrong.
You're not just wrong, you're soft,
which comes of living in too many places,
taking too much heed of other people.
You have to live among your own, it's a life's
work just understanding what it means
to be from here
                 —by which I mean
right here, right now. Forget photography
that makes you laugh at how you used to look.
That's what's so good about tattoos.
It hurts to have your elbow webbed, your neck
marked with the swift off the *Swift* matchbox,
but when you've had it done it's done for life.
It's a commitment, like a marriage.
It's just like being married to yourself.

Neanderthal Funeral

sunlight on the ice sheet a shower of rain driven before it a rainbow then sun again on moraine on this place lets call it carryduff lets call it mountstewart i wish i could do more than these few flowers camomile daisies peethebeds ive never been up to the challenge blue plastic carrier round your wee scrap of blanket that used to be mine and i still like to feel it near me so at least im giving you something that means something im giving you something i love nearly as much as i wouldve loved you you tiny surprise you gift you glacier

Skateboarders near St. Anne's Cathedral, Belfast

You curse these snails whose aerosols and magic
markers leave this spoor along the concrete,
their script more arabic than roman, curlicues
of codewords, slogans, tags and monikers.
You'd like to blame them for the broken windows
in that unlet office, but their baggy shorts, their *Vans*
are innocent. Their shelty forelocks mark them out
as Yeatsians, inept and tranced, our last romantics.
Look at them scoot. A few yards of smooth-as-ice-cream
motion, then they try some kick-flip or wheelie
or one-eighty and it all goes skewwhiff. It's beast,
so lighten up. Try to find a grain of sympathy
for each talentless, aspirational Sisyphus
who lifts his battered board up by its trucks, pretending
to ignore the girls who blank him while he tries again
the simple-looking stunt that seems to be beyond
the best of his abilities, if not his dreams.

Welcome to Dry City

It's a big ten-four
to the man with the famous handle
and the puffy face braving
a wind that would cut you,
the smell of the fish factory
and the sandblasted foreshore
at Cloghy or Cloughey,
however they spell it.

Two decades ago
there wasn't a pub for miles
on this redneck coast.
It's still a far cry
from Fulham Broadway
and the old crack about models and fizz
in hotel jacuzzis—
So, George, where did it all go wrong?

A quick dash through the caravan park
and another half-one
for the famous blow-in
with the weepy eyes.
Let the *Telegraph* snapper
stalk the bleak carpark
where the bollards
are red, white and blue

and the gannets squabble—
breaker, breaker—
over half a battered sausage
and a gravy chip.
He's no liver specialist
but even to him
the bad taste in his mouth—
acid, fish and ashes—

is clear as *Smirnoff*
and the gut-ache's pure
homesickness, a geographical.
Which is how you might
translate the word
nostalgia: the slow nod
to the landlord's *Have youse
no homes to go to?*

Tractatus

His throat is bandaged to the chin.
He can't pay for his drinks.
People avoid him, but for the base
misshapen fans he sponges off
he means the world and, as he shrinks,
the world is everything that is the case.

Taller on television, holding the baby
like a winner's cheque, he stood
for possibility: you could take the boy
out of Belfast *and* Belfast out of the boy.
A man could make it on his tod.
Now he's a death's-head drawn by Rowell Friers.
What can be shown cannot be said.

Read about Ireland's Highest Pub
i.m. James Simmons

>Crossing the country after your funeral,
>I break my journey at the Ponderosa
>and contemplate roadkill: not
>those cats and foxes, but the birds
>(starlings, sparrows, crows and magpies too)
>whose wings flex up from their remains
>as if the tarmac'd grown them, or
>the roads of Ireland were about to rise
>up from their beds of soil and hard core
>like a flock of—no, like oil-stained angels.

Ice
i.m. Paddy McArdle

When morphine constipates him
a neighbour tells him ice will free his bowels.
His wife feeds ice-cubes one by one
inside him, till at last he squeezes out
a tiny, blood-dark, frozen stool—

ice, mostly, though his belly feels
like it's still hard-pressed snow, a chunk
of pack-ice frozen to his spine.
Another patient at the hospice tells him,

'If it wasn't for the call of nature, some
of us would never walk again.'

The Spear

When the conversation swerved from marriage
breakdowns to Golding's *Lord of the Flies*,
we were drunk stroke stoned enough to realise
that each of us was Ralph, but Jack as well ...
At some stage you went out into the shed
and came back with this cherished boyhood relic—
fifteen feet of homemade bamboo fishing spear,
a six-inch nail filed to a barbed harpoon-
point at the tip—and mourned the flatfish
shoals that used to crowd our inshore waters.
Hard to believe how long ago it was
you used to pluck them from the sea like stones.
How easily they came. How lost they are.

For Thoth

In a stonemasons' yard behind Whitehead station,
they're engraving pillars for some Belgian theme-bar,
or at least when I asked them that's what I was told:
'An Egyptian theme-bar, mate, all obelisks.'
They're carving ankhs and scarabs, in some red,
friable-looking rock like Scrabo sandstone,
chiselling pharaonic profiles, hawk-
and cat- and dog-head gods whose grins suggest
that life can't be all bad when you can greet
your fellow human beings with the question:
'Well boys, are youse still at the hieroglyphics?'

Wind Farm

The elegant slim towers of a wind farm
on the Antrim skyline, happier than pylons
or thoroughbreds, the triple-bladed rotors
diffident, precise, as poets on their first glass.

Ringtones

In the land of Cockaigne across the border
you can have 'Come As You Are' or 'Smoke on the Water',
'You'll Never Walk Alone' or 'If I Were a Rich Man'.
Coming from Lurgan, though, you're bound to pick
'When Irish Eyes Are Smiling', 'The Black Velvet Band',
'Cockles and Musseles' (sic) or 'Mountains of the Mourne' (sic).

The Wreck of the Mobile Library

Mills & Boon, large
print for the housebound,
travel guides, very little
that you'd call literature:

when my foot sank into
the mud of the wrong pedal
and I mounted the kerb,
it all took wing swiftly.

My windscreen's broken.
Who'd guess that paperbacks
had such momentum?
Headlight-glass and pages

litter wet tarmac, dust-
jackets flex in slipstream.
Here's me with a buckled axle,
an hour's wait for a towtruck.

I used to park by the sea
and scribble poems. No more.
Adorno on first drafts:
'organised self-deception.'

My boss on the phone later:
'The bus is totalled.
I couldn't put a price on all
the books you've ruined.'

Swarfega

So they gave you all cartridge pens. For weeks
you'd come home with hands stained as the butcher's
of some indigo-blooded animal.
Or the summer sun liquified the tar
on carpark surfaces, bitumen wept
on telegraph poles, and you'd trail it in
on hands and feet. Nothing for it but your
da's *Swarfega*. You stood there, hands a bowl,
your mother'd crack the tin with a green pre-
decimal penny or a screwdriver
and spoon the purplish slime into your palms
like jam, with the sound of one hand clapping
once. 'Rub,' she'd say, but what she meant was, grind
that glaar into every stained pore, wring
your little hands like some Dickensian
worrier, some Fagin. This was one thing
you couldn't overdo. You'd seen your da's
own two-fisted kneading of the ultra-
violet slop, that plumped into the sink
with paint-flecks suspended in its slaver.
Now it's your own hands in the cleansing jelly,
you listening to that slurp, that sex-noise.
You think: I should put on music for this,
Bob Marley, maybe, and 'Redemption Song',
but just keep looking at your hands, all Xd
and Vd like the Martian crust, grime ingrained
in every hack, pore and hangnail. 'I
know it like the back of my hand,' you say,
meaning your own room, your town, your life ...
but it's only now you see them, in their
true weathered nature, coming clean at last—
skin and knucklebone, old burn scars, the tip
of a thumb that went under the hammer
and came out flattened. You hold them up
to your face and think: I could eat off them.
You stare at them and think: They look half-eaten.

Peter Quince

It was the high point of my life, of all our lives,
our one chance to get shot of the nine-to-five.

Says me to Bottom and Snout, 'After tomorrow,
jack in the day job. Be like scooping the lotto ... '

But none of them took me seriously enough
to be themselves. The lot of them acted up,

that waster Bottom most of all. 'A pint or two,'
he said, 'to steady my nerves.' The rest you know:

blotto on stage, talking back to the upper-crust,
full of himself, big-headed, but embarrassed

at the same time, which put the rest of us off ...
We took a fearful heckling from the toffs,

who buggered off with catcalls, jeers and whistles.
All I could see was sawdust and blunt chisels.

Packing our props away, I kept it zipped.
I wanted them to think I didn't care, but flipped,

threatening them all with hammers, saws and blades
when Starveling said, 'Least we've still got our trades.'

Money

Money, my landlady, counts the towels and keys.
The pink blade of soap in her bathroom smells
of old hospital. Money begrudges a second
rasher at breakfast, and serves me an itemised bill.

Money takes it for granted I'm a pervert or thief.
No visitors after nine, and no girls in the room at all.
I don't tell anyone where I live. I can't tell whether
it's me who's ashamed of money, or money of me.

Marriage

The couple were found by their children in separate rooms,
each missing a limb, each kitchen-knifed more than once—
in the chest, in the eyes, in the mouth, in the foot, in the groin—
detectives are looking for nobody else in connection ...

Criticism

It's that woman Elizabeth Bishop again
with her diffident whimpers
about life, how difficult yet lovely
our countries are. I'm sick of it.
What gives her the right to come round
here stammering about journeys
I don't even believe she's taken? Give me
Robert Lowell any day, or my three-
year-old daughter who said, straight
off the bus from Boston to Franconia,
'Dad, I *love* American darkness.'

Toilet Training

Jack has taken five years to reach
this moment of priapic bafflement,
his eyes shut, hair plastered in sweat,
about to piss on the landing. Which
he has done before—who hasn't?
I take him to the toilet, pull pyjamas
down, and point his rigid nozzle at
the water in the bowl. Hypnopompic
mutterer, he sways like a drunk.
His hard-on the size of my little finger
won't fold away after it's shaken
but makes a tent of his pyjama-bottoms
and steers him, just as I do, back to bed—
male and disoriented, one of the led.

Pet World

Ellen is bored by the rodent-tunnels
where tremulous fur's asleep, a rumour
among shit and brittle shavings.
She grazes each terrarium briefly,
arriving suddenly at the aisle's mouth
where a garish bird won't speak, songbirds
punily lord it on dry twigs or fritter
in whispers over sour cage floors
and where my son—dayglo neon
shrapnel in the acquaria, biblical
pillars of bubbles—presses his slick palms
to something even uglier than God
that's suckered to the glass: genital eye,
dissected muscle, pallid foetal dragon.

Special Needs

'What age are you? Which colour is red?
Where is the girl who was here yesterday?
Is this all right? Is this? What time is it?'

Repeat, with variations. Angela fidgets
from question to question, concentrates
for a nanosecond, then loses the thread.

Except that it was never hers to lose:
'What time is it? Which is blue? Is this all right?
Where is the girl who was here yesterday?'

The Reconstruction

Twenty-five, and mutton dressed as lamb,
she walks the shopping street in children's clothes.
Nobody's memory's jogged. The kid
she's trying to impersonate's
long dead. Search parties comb
huge fields of rape like absent-minded
people looking for a watch, a pair of specs,
a key. What does she think
she's doing: making up for wasted time,
a misspent youth? Nobody's taken in.
This is the youngest she will ever be.

The Gallery of Anxiety Will be Closing Shortly

Patrons are asked to find the exit for themselves.
Security cannot be reached on the usual extensions.
Another cup of coffee is the last thing I want,
the last thing I need, but I'll collapse without one.

This would not be happening to Martine,
who does not drink or tell lies, or if she does
is not caught out, or if she is will just uncup
a breast and set the nipple to your lips.

What I think she means is 'Be content with
what is nearly true—better that than have me
show the police that snapshot of your father
in his uniform, a number scribbled on the back.

Better that than have it public knowledge.'

Why Not Slaughter Your Whole Family?

Whatever you do, put nothing on paper.
The children who're sleeping with one hot cheek
exposed to the breath you hold
                          have only

one hope of salvation; the love of your life
asleep in the room down the landing
has only one hope.

                      The hammer, the chainsaw
you keep for the hedge, the polythene bags
you bring home with the shopping, the pills—

the everyday world supplies all you could need,
cures for the comforts of adulthood,
charms against safety.

                Of course
they are angels in gold leaf, but listen to me:
I am the Bible, I am your conscience,

I am the internet, I am the muse
of the cellular telephone mast in the playground
signalling via your microwave oven.

I am the genome, the autopsy tapes
and nothing I say can be safely
                        committed to writing.

The Cancellation of the Races
for David Crystal

When grass is left unscythed
on Chepstow, Market Rasen,
and the water in the water-jump
grows reeds and wading birds
scoop frogspawn from its sludge
(because the day is coming

when the stable boys grow old
in idleness, the jockeys fat,
the owners gone to cockfights
out by Neasden, when the nags
are children's pets or company
for cattle torched on sleepers)

and when the cashier's left
his window out of boredom
we will still gnaw stubby pens
under the blank TVs awaiting
the outcome of accumulators
placed when we were young

(because it won't be long
before our coteries are scouring
Britain for a working bookie,
all our money on a rank outsider,
ankle-deep in butts and beaten
dockets) when we'd shirts

to lose on tips from tabloid
racing pages left behind on trains
when railways worked, when form
was still a kind of oracle or omen
promising if not the earth
at least enough of it to live on.

One Man Show

I
Seated female nude with map of Co. Antrim

> Your arms are folded over your breasts.
> The contours of hip and buttock catch
> the edge of the light that plunges across
> Glenoe, Kilwaughter, Ballynure—
> but it's not the map you study. Your face
> is turned to the left, the red in your hair
> takes on a violent life of its own, a private
> energy. The wall behind you is brick,
> as naked and unforthcoming as yourself.
> A mirror hung there shows your glacial back.

II
Reclining female nude with agricultural implements

> As if you meant to see off all-comers
> or stood for death in an allegorical print,
> you lie with a scythe in your arms
> like a skinny lover. The curve of the blade
> behind your neck mirrors the sweep
> of a strong white leg across the haft.
> A quernstone lies at the foot of the bed,
> a churn stands at the head, where a book
> or glass of wine on a night table might
> seem more appropriate. In shadow,
> a pitchfork and a spool of new barbed wire.
> A *Thompson's* feed bag like discarded underwear.

III
Still life with surgical apparatus

> The titanium framework of a surgical brace
> bright on the worktop's granite-effect
> and heat-resistant melamine. Strip-light

glances off a bonesaw, floods
the plaster-and-resin cast of a male torso:
a cuirass, a corset for an injured back
unzipped at one side and marked with a cross
at the fifth lumbar vertebra, in Prussian blue.

IV
Figures in a landscape

In this pastiche of *Le Déjeuner sur L'Herbe*
the men wear overalls, the woman hunkers
above a dictionary of Ulster-Scots
and a ball of baling twine. Tempestuous skies
carry a squadron of gulls and a limb
of amber smoke from a chimney on fire
in Ballycarry, near the grave of Orr
who mocked the uxurious rebels who fled
the yeomanry for the opulent flesh
of their wives, and their wives' warm beds.

V
Portrait of the artist's wife with dismantled motorcycle

Though you're fully dressed—a trouser suit
in business black, black shoes and shirt—
the motorcycle parts around your feet remind
the eye of buttocks, breasts and hips,
the curve of arm or leg. As if you'd burst
from the carapace of the robot in *Metropolis*
or given up the armoured life of Joan,
the metal forms recall your body and
fetishise renounced desire.
You hold a spark-plug in your open hand.

The Naachtun Stela: Inscriptions in Time of Civil War

Glyphs for thunder and alligators, corn and breath.
It could be a prayer, it could be banal
journalese. It could be a memo-to-self.

The priest-king pierces his scrotum, his earlobe.
What kind of graffito is this? His queen
drags a rope of thorns through her own tongue.

A worker-elite of plasterers, painters made these.
Are they dirty pictures? Are they doodles?
Me, I'm doomed to live on monkey and be baffled.

Fever Diet #2
from the archives of the Royal Victoria Hospital, Belfast

If the hospital be not
    for the reception of the poor,
        he for one knew not its intention

My arm, sir, was caught
    in a hackling machine,
        and it drew the sinews out of it
nearly a yard long

    his hands and face
        were blue as indigo

The hospital is now open
    for the reception
        of respectable strangers

If the hospital be not
    for the reception of the poor

    cut it off
with a pair of scissors
    and then held it up

    Resolution:—
That no bodies found dead
    be admitted into the hospital

    If the hospital be not
for the reception

    no burnt children were allowed to remain

    me go no more to Riga

Twenty-eight contusions,
  five injuries to the eye,

       one injury by explosion of gunpowder,
thirty-eight fractures,
  eighteen scalp wounds,

       six immersions,
twenty-five lacerated wounds,
  two wounds of throat

       (suicidal),
one incised wound,
  one punctured wound,

       five poisoning cases,
one wound of vein,
  and two dislocations.

       If the hospital be not

Antiquities
from the archaeological exhibition at Belfast, September 1852

IN CASE 9

    A Felt Hat, found sixteen feet deep in a bog,
and the skull of Carolan, a celebrated Irish Bard.

IN CASE 26

    An ancient brass Ecclesiastical seal. A Smoking-Pipe. Also, an ancient iron Penance-Girdle.

MISCELLANEOUS OBJECTS

    Branks: the ancient Scotch or English instrument
of punishment for scolding women.

    Two three-pronged wooden Implements,
long-handled, probably agricultural, found in a bog.

IN CASE 16

    An American Indian Arrow-head of flint, with which the late
Dr. Gillmer, of Dromore, was wounded in the leg.

IN RECESS 2

    Five querns, of various forms. Two human bones.

IN CASE 12

    A remarkable and unique bronze Instrument,

    at one end a double hook, and at the other a ring and swivel.
The stem of the Instrument is perforated

    with seven holes, through each of which passes a wire,
terminated at the top by a figure or a bird,

    and at the bottom by a loose ring. The stem is hollow.
When found it contained a portion of an oaken rod,

curiously inlaid with thin laminae of brass.
No satisfactory use has been assigned for this item

formerly in the collection of the late Bishop
of Down, Connor and Dromore, and found in a bog.

from *The Epic of Gilgamesh*: Enkidu's Dream

I had another dream last night:
while the land between the rivers was in uproar,
I stood buck-naked before a sour-faced
and austere black bird, a kind of puritan eagle.
He went for me, all claws,
and as those talons throttled me
I saw my arms sprout feathers just like his,
saw them translated into scrawny wings.

Then he carried me off to a pitch-black house
where the dead all sat like starving birds
eating the dust off the earthen floor.
They were feathered like me,
even the dead kings. Those who'd held court
like gods now bowed and scraped,
no better than lackeys who fetch and carry
meat and water for the Queen of the Dead—

or her bookkeeper, who asked my name
and scratched it into clay, her script
like the prints birds leave in drying mud.
Gilgamesh, my card was marked.
I felt like a bankrupt in the grip
of bailiffs, asset-stripped, foreclosed.
My empty belly retched and heaved.
Take it from me, my days are numbered.

March 2003

The Last Poem

's strangled at birth
with a cable stripped
from the last ship named
at Harland & Wolff.

All that is left
of the dead Island language
is *Garmoyle* and *Dargan*.
(The spellcheck insists

on *gargoyle* and *dragon*.)
The incompetent shade
of Thomas Carnduff
snarls burly doggerel

while posed in his Sash
on the Linen Hall roof.
This printer's devil
turned Rotten Prod

in an archipelago
of bankrupt shipyards
says: bite your tongue.
The *Magheramorne*

Manifesto's
as good as a nod
to the land's minor poets
and major fools.

The choice, in Belfast
as elsewhere, 's between
being made redundant
and downing tools.